I0617507

H-5.7.5-192

Written By
Michael Irvin Walker

Haikus By Michael Irvin Walker

<u>H-5.7.5-192</u>

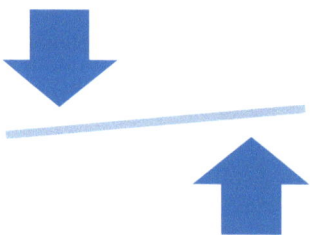

PROLOGUE

Due to belief in freedom of expression in creativity and free speech, I offer the following.

CAVEAT:

contains explicit and sexual language

contains misogyny

NOTE BEFORE JUDGEMENT

Snoop Dogg is misogynistic IN SONG

Snoop Dogg is 27 Years
A Husband/Father IN LIFE

Haikus By Michael Irvin Walker

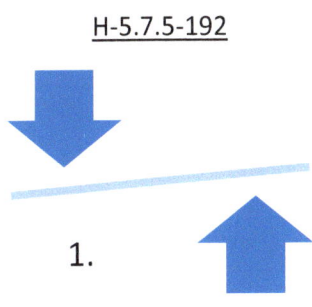

1.

Damn, look at her ass

I wonder just possibly

Can I get in it

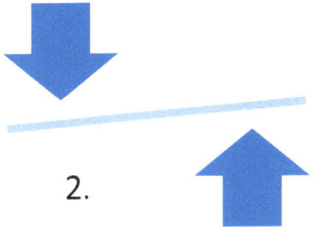

2.

When I was a teen

Being a drug dealer was

Just the thing to do

Haikus By Michael Irvin Walker

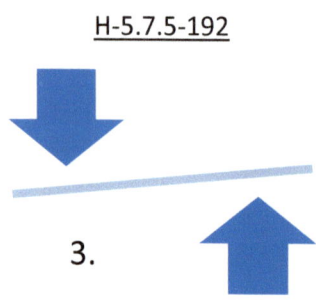

3.

You want to test Lyte

What are you stupid or just

Out of your damn mind

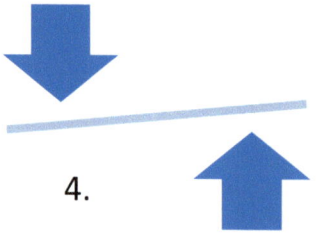

4.

Ralph stores are so near

You can't help but get fat so

Fuck it smoke weed too

Haikus By Michael Irvin Walker

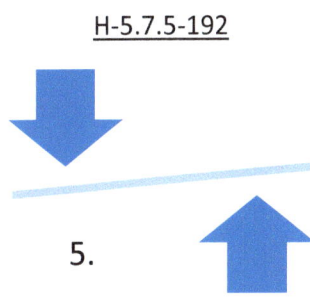

5.

As the day turns night

I'm in Malibu thinking

Will I marry who

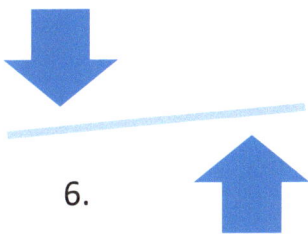

6.

Fuck you you bitch ass

I'll knock yo fuckin' teeth out

Now say some moe shit

Haikus By Michael Irvin Walker

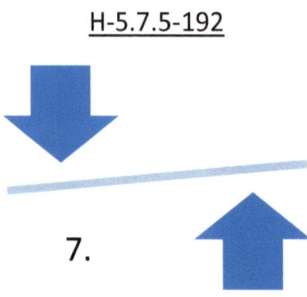

7.

Marina del rey

Can't think what to say about

Marina del rey

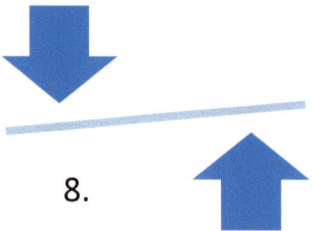

8.

Wake up my dick hard

Give me some wet pussy now

Thanks hoe tramp bitch slut

Haikus By Michael Irvin Walker

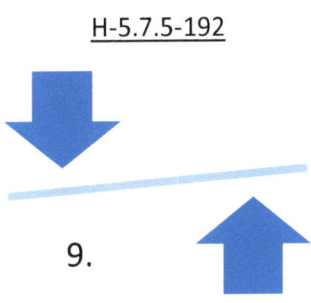

9.

When I suck your soul

You scream like nobody else

That's why I love you

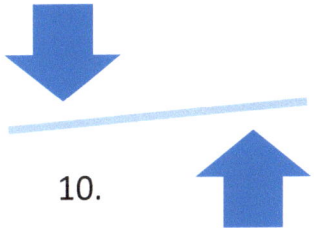

10.

What was thinking he

Maybe thinking he was not

So that's what they thought

Haikus By Michael Irvin Walker

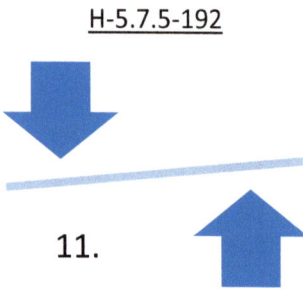

11.

Power of pussy

It can make you lose your mind

It wins all the time

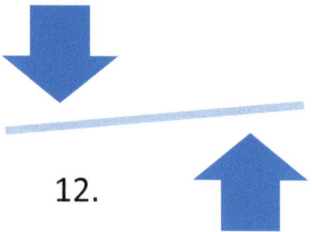

12.

Prince what a rock star

Make your girl cum in panties

Prince what the hell man

Haikus By Michael Irvin Walker

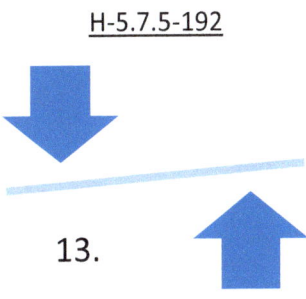

13.

Write with a blue pen

I don't know why I said that

Langston Huges was gay

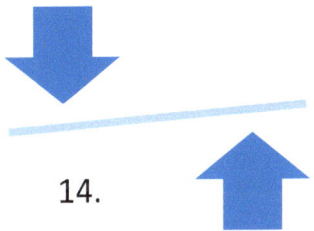

14.

Blessed be not depressed

My mom used to say that shit

Well I ain't either

Haikus By Michael Irvin Walker

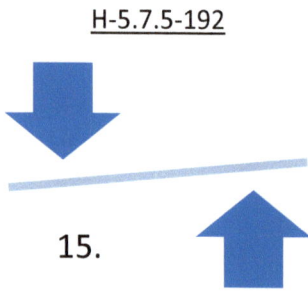

15.

Your pussy stank hoe

I can't stand a stank pussy

But you still fucked it

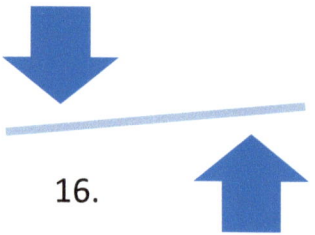

16.

To figure out life

Why the fuck would you do that

Just roll with the shit

Haikus By Michael Irvin Walker

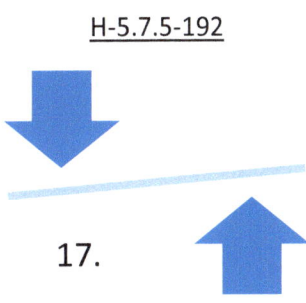

17.

Ego humbleness

Those are the keys to this life

So be humble bitch

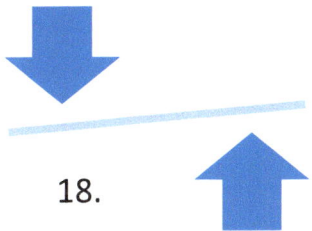

18.

Procrastination

Tergiversation that is

Will kill ambition

Haikus By Michael Irvin Walker

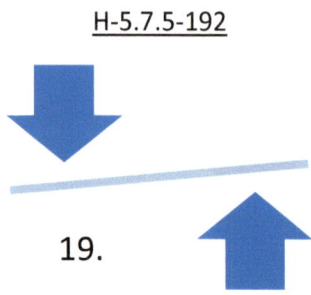

19.

Wish I was famous

Why you ask do I want that

Jay Z fucks the world

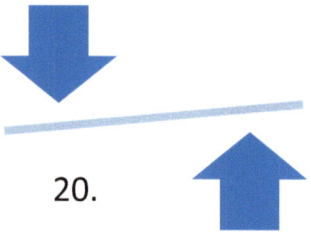

20.

You're such an asshole

Fuck you suck my dick too bitch

You see what I mean

Haikus By Michael Irvin Walker

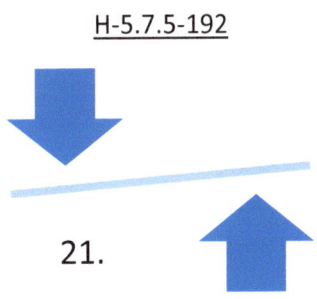

21.

Either you roll on

Or you just get rolled over

It's just that simple

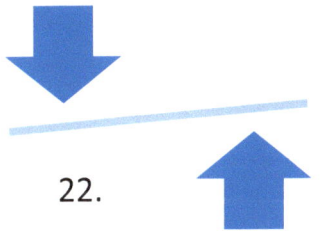

22.

Either you create

Or you die a nobody

Better get busy

Haikus By Michael Irvin Walker

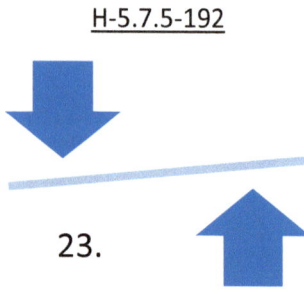

23.

Cinco De Mayo

But fuck I'm not Mexican

It don't matter drink

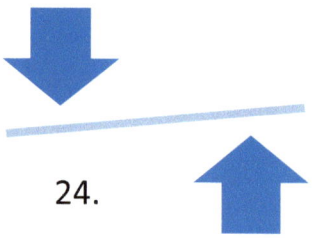

24.

My name is D-Nice

Club Quarantine is my thing

Corona Virus

Haikus By Michael Irvin Walker

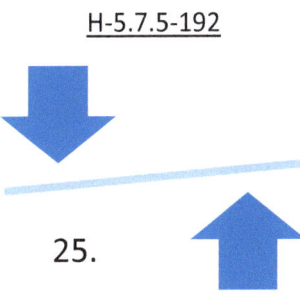

25.

Please tease me tonight

Want to love you all over

Want to bring you joy

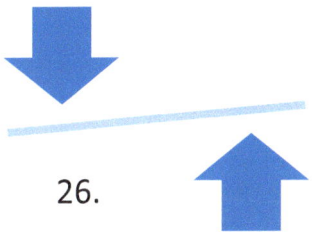

26.

Are you a jealous

There's no need to be jealous

It is a weakness

Haikus By Michael Irvin Walker

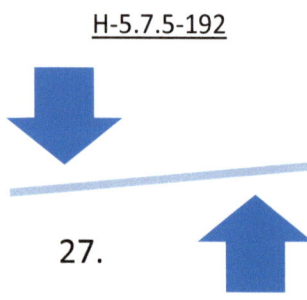

27.

No negative shit

But life is negative right

Well, maybe you're right

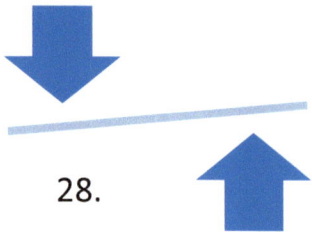

28.

All the feels in here

Because I'm thinking of you

I'm in ecstasy

Haikus By Michael Irvin Walker

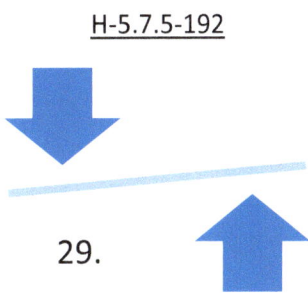

29.

Give me a soul clap

What up Andre The Giant

Hip Hop Forever

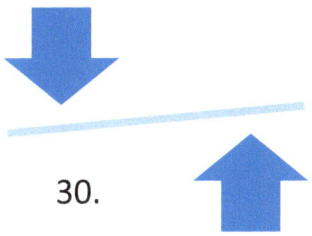

30.

That's easier said

But to do it takes a lot

You're so negative

Haikus By Michael Irvin Walker

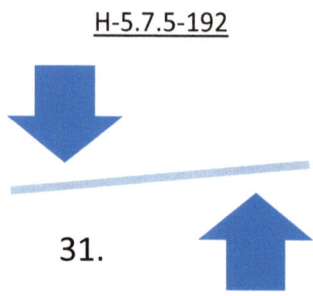

31.

Middle of the night

When creative spark happens

Sleep is deaths' cousin

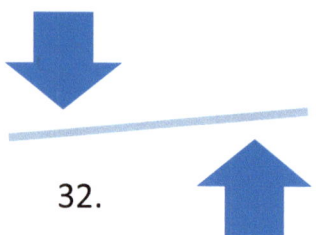

32.

I am creative

But I don't get paid for it

Tired of this shit

Haikus By Michael Irvin Walker

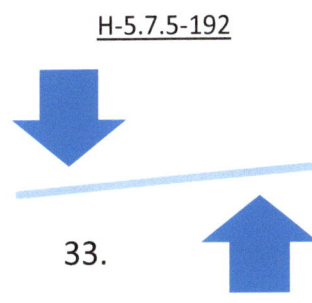

33.

I am a rapper

But shouldn't you retire

Fuck that I can rap

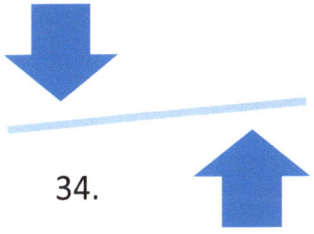

34.

She suck your dick good

How you gon' resist those lips

Oh fellatio

Haikus By Michael Irvin Walker

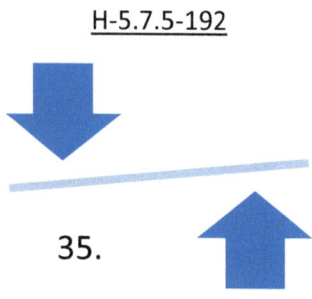

35.

It's She Real Hip Hop

Straight from Harlem NYC

A lyrical bitch

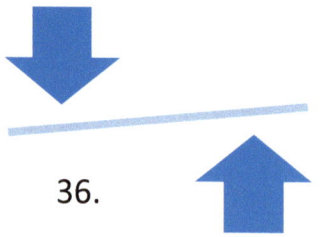

36.

What is a haiku

Just seventeen syllables

Kind of weird though right

Haikus By Michael Irvin Walker

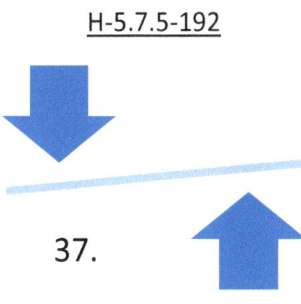

37.

Do you have the gall

Ain't no shook hands in Brooklyn

Pray for my downfall

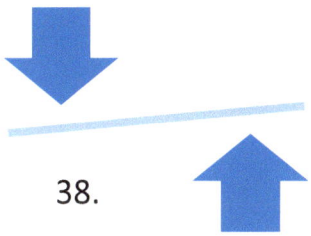

38.

Michael I Walker

A higher fucking level

Hey what can I say

Haikus By Michael Irvin Walker

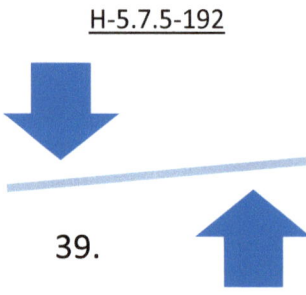

39.

It's good to be Black

It's such a beautiful day

In Black neighborhoods

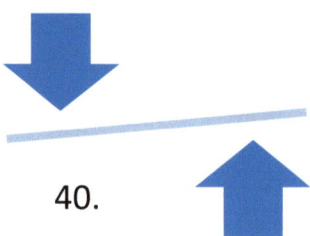

40.

We tired of y'all

Why won't you stop killing us

We tried! FUCK THIS! POW!

Haikus By Michael Irvin Walker

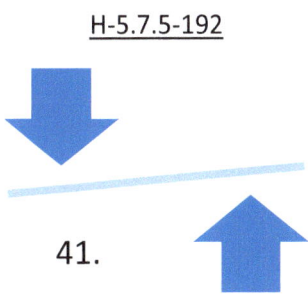

41.

I'll make you holla

Make you wanna go crazy

That's what this dick do

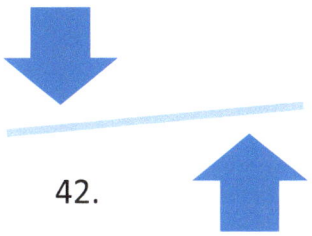

42.

When I saw you first

The most beautifullest thing

I still remember

Haikus By Michael Irvin Walker

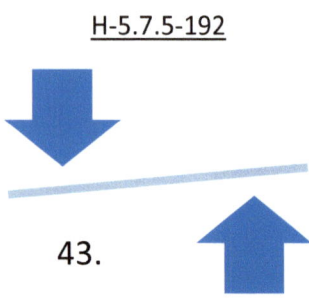

43.

You are bored as fuck

Leave that job you have to do

Just let it go man

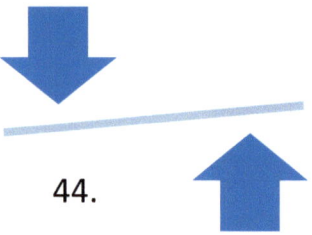

44.

Who's Valentina

She such a beautiful site

That's Valentina

Haikus By Michael Irvin Walker

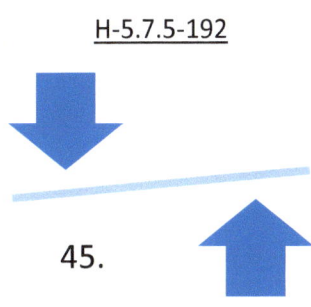

45.

Said to me don't rap

I said to her I am rap

I want a divorce

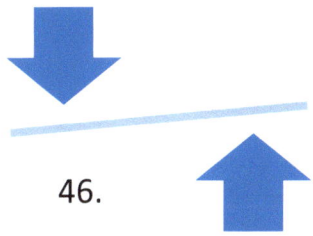

46.

This dog won't shut up

Wish I could close its mouth shut

He is such a bitch

Haikus By Michael Irvin Walker

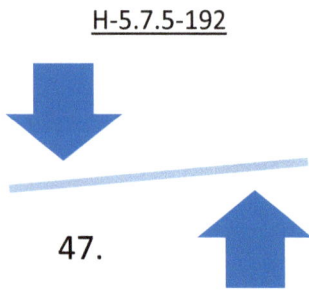

47.

What you lookin' at

I'll fuck you up bitch nigga

Look at me again

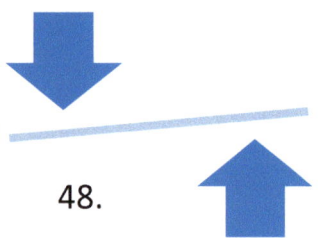

48.

Loriale Daughter

I'm gon' slap the shit out her

Little ingrate bitch

Haikus By Michael Irvin Walker

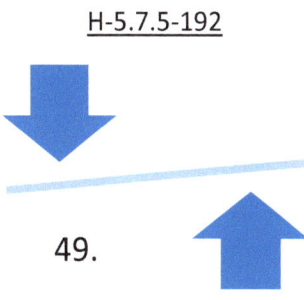

49.

What is the purpose

None just live in the moment

Smoke weed sniff cocaine

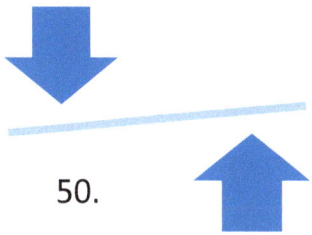

50.

You have work to do

Stop fucking around and work

You lethargic bitch

Haikus By Michael Irvin Walker

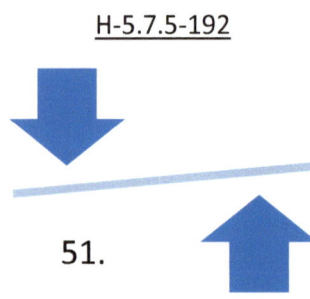

51.

Social media

You social media whore

You are fake famous

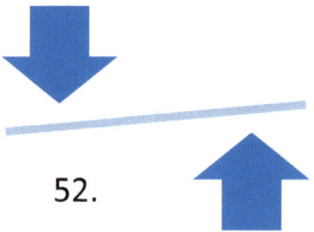

52.

You are not a star

You will never be a star

Stop with the bullshit

Haikus By Michael Irvin Walker

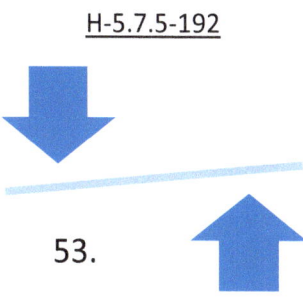

53.

School Daze Malcolm X

Do The Right Thing He Got Game

Spike culture icon

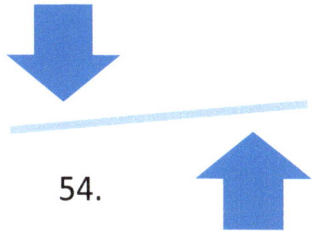

54.

Shoot one moe Blackman

Going on a killing spree

We tried to tell y'all

Haikus By Michael Irvin Walker

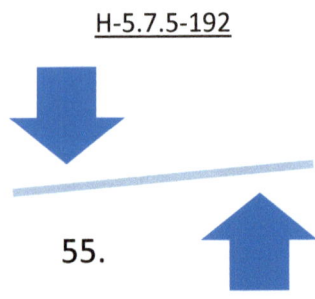

55.

Hope he cheat on you

You left me for his money

Hope he goes to jail

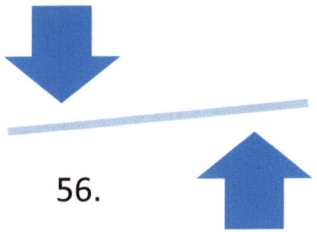

56.

Hope your dick fall off

Wish prostate cancer on you

You cheated on me

Haikus By Michael Irvin Walker

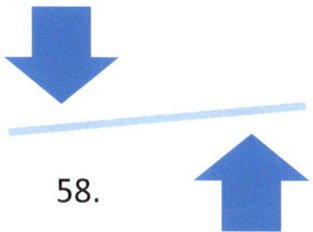

57.

Shift alt control "F"

Wonderful program excel

Copy paste group sum

58.

Don't have to get fat

You just have to exercise

You sloven disgust

Haikus By Michael Irvin Walker

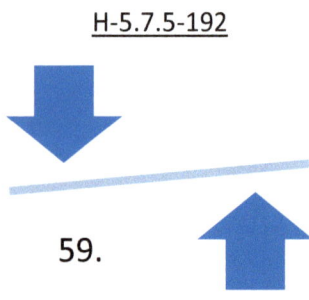

59.

Corona Virus

American idiots

They buy what is sold

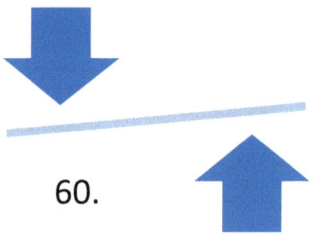

60.

Asymptomatic

That is a bunch of bullshit

But you believe them

Haikus By Michael Irvin Walker

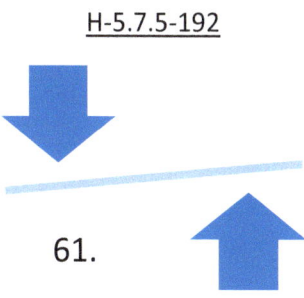

61.

Women are bullshit

If you love them they complain

Smack them they complain

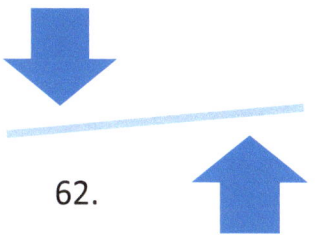

62.

I don't give a fuck

Can't beat them and can't join them

Fuck that shit just live

Haikus By Michael Irvin Walker

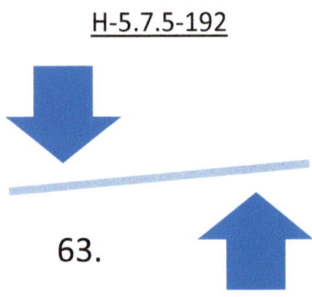

63.

Black people don't talk

Lack of emotions training

But they sho mo-shno

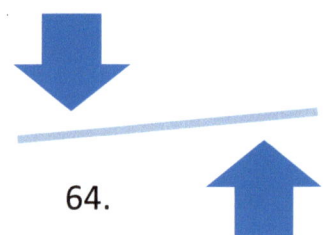

64.

Covid shut shit down

I travelled and created

Covid won't stop me

Haikus By Michael Irvin Walker

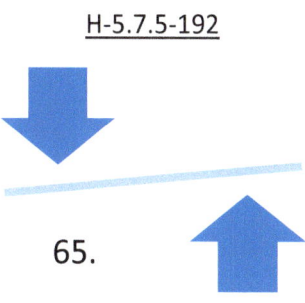

65.

I'm so high right now

I may write the best haiku

Which will say eat ass

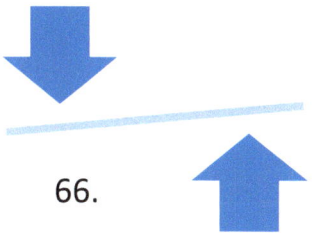

66.

Two ways to do things

Michaels' way and the wrong way

Just gotta believe

Haikus By Michael Irvin Walker

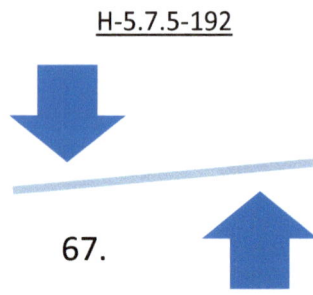

67.

All you have to do

Eat healthy and exercise

Love Diabetes

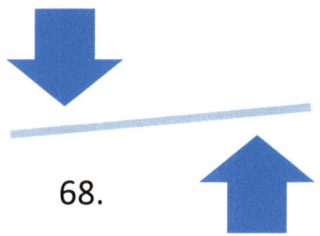

68.

No to joe biden

A bullshit politician

That is what I said

Haikus By Michael Irvin Walker

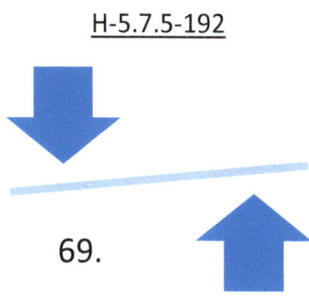

69.

When you take the time

To do something good for life

That's living the dream

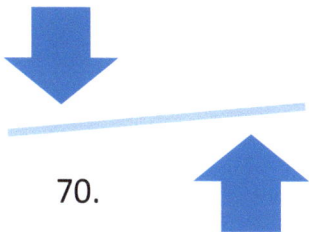

70.

Eat drink shit fuck sleep

That is the science of life

What more can I say

Haikus By Michael Irvin Walker

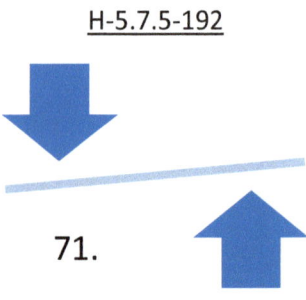

71.

Dreams do not come true

Actions will bring a result

Act and don't worry

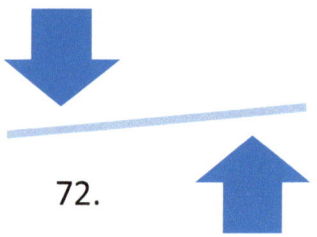

72.

How are you doing

Great I'm white and kill black men

Don't get no better

Haikus By Michael Irvin Walker

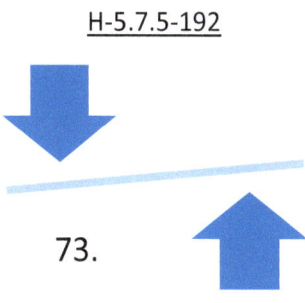

73.

Get high in Cali

Just like when in Amsterdam

Cali Amsterdam

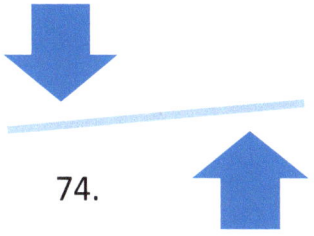

74.

Black people and spades

White people they call it hearts

It's all just card games

Haikus By Michael Irvin Walker

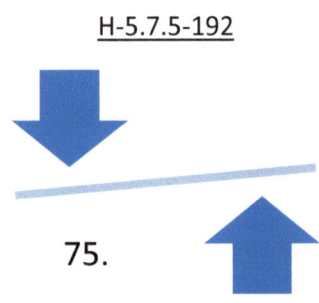

75.

The Michael Jordan

Greatest basketball player

LeBron James will…. Not

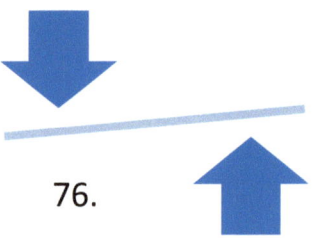

76.

LeBron James is great

Greater than Michael Jordan

He will never be

Haikus By Michael Irvin Walker

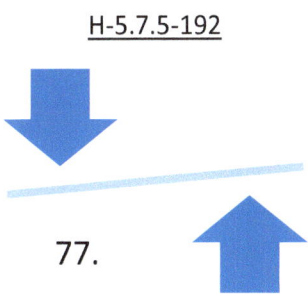

77.

This todays' Haiku

I'm sick of the fucking shit

That's all for today

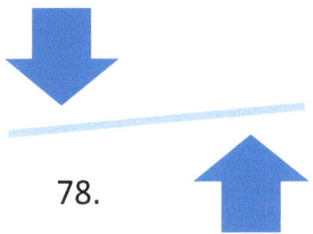

78.

You're league M.V.P.

Michael Jordan says bullshit

Who won the series

Haikus By Michael Irvin Walker

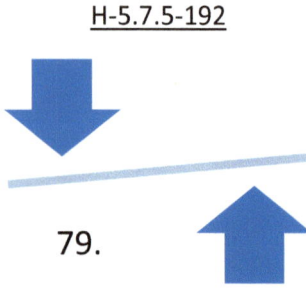

79.

Jordans' the last dance

Who will ever be greater

No fucking body

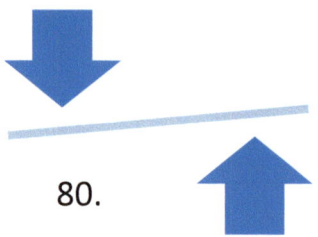

80.

To win something is

One of the greatest feelings

No doubt about that

Haikus By Michael Irvin Walker

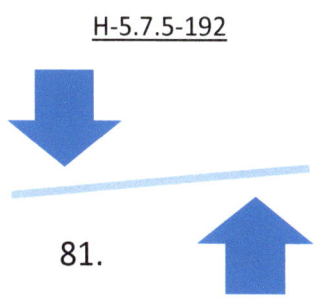

81.

We were better team

Reggie Miller would say so

But didn't beat bulls

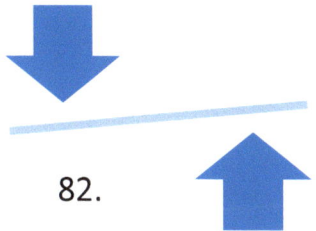

82.

Live in the moment

No worries of tomorrow

I've been born again

Haikus By Michael Irvin Walker

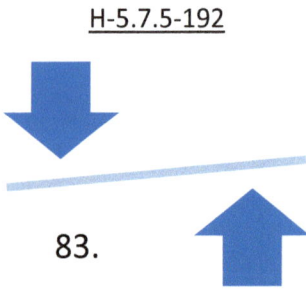

83.

What is it with this

This the confederate flag

It is not racist

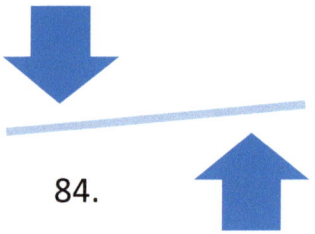

84.

You my family

Only one who give a fuck

Sorry you're fired

Haikus By Michael Irvin Walker

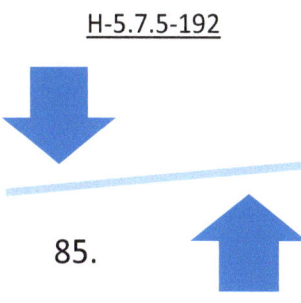

85.

Life is not that fair

Sometimes you take a beating

Everyone gets beat

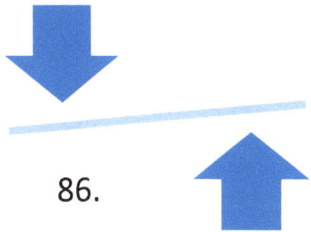

86.

The bars are open

Covid-19 go away

Sick of in the house

Haikus By Michael Irvin Walker

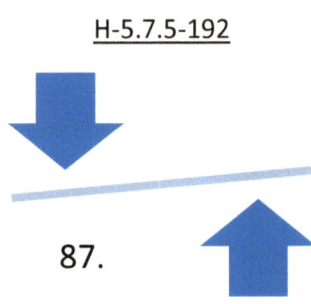

87.

I am a rich man

Food clothing shelter and sleep

That is all I need

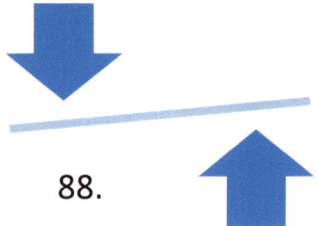

88.

You want to get high

Try smoking crack rock cocaine

There goes your whole life

Haikus By Michael Irvin Walker

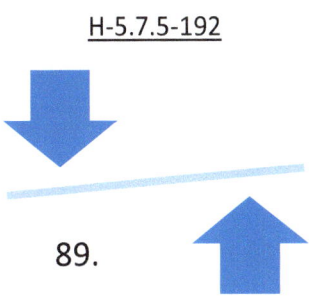

89.

Atlanta Georgia

Home of black girl big asses

Home of black gay men

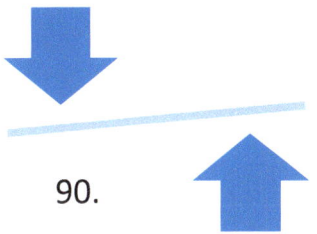

90.

In Mississippi

Spending time with family

What a great feeling

Haikus By Michael Irvin Walker

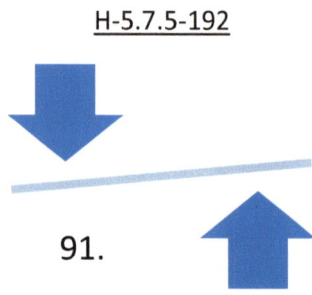

91.

I'm going down south

To Moorhead Mississippi

To Roxanna May

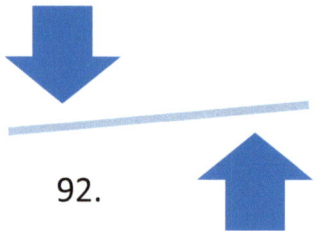

92.

At my cousin house

Hattiesburg Mississippi

That is where I'm at

Haikus By Michael Irvin Walker

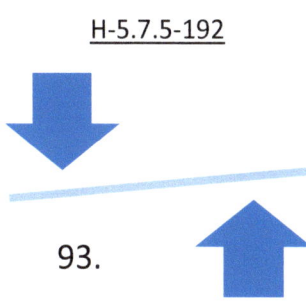

93.

I'm in Belzoni

It's the catfish capital

Ole Mississippi

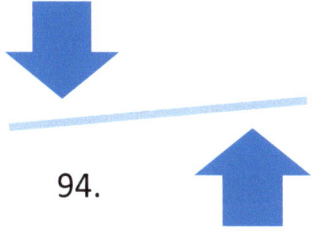

94.

Indianola

This is where my roots started

In Mississippi

Haikus By Michael Irvin Walker

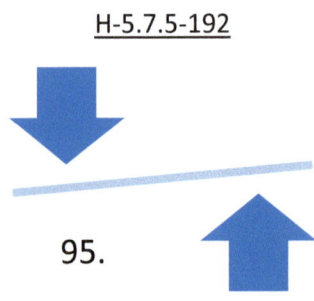

95.

On the road again

Inverness Mississippi

Ever heard of it

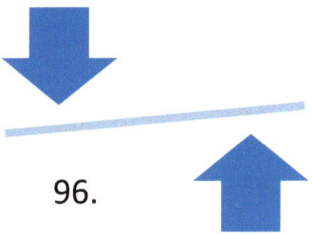

96.

Martin Luther King

Against the real life devil

j. edgar hoover

Haikus By Michael Irvin Walker

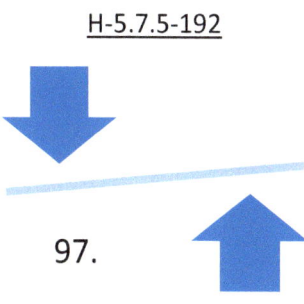

97.

Sunflower County

That's where my people are from

Ole Mississippi

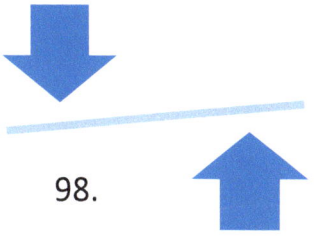

98.

That is Donald Trump

Ego is out of control

White privileged rich

Haikus By Michael Irvin Walker

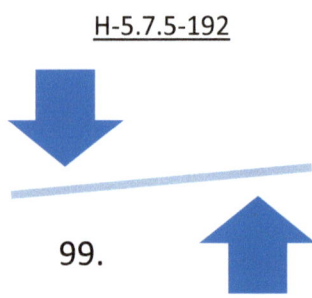

99.

Hit the lottery

Buy a bunch of shit go broke

That's living the dream

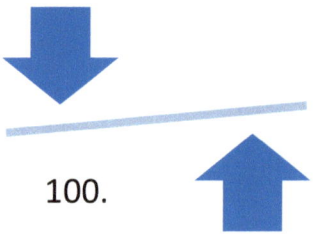

100.

I am gaining weight

Corona virus bullshit

The gyms are all closed

Haikus By Michael Irvin Walker

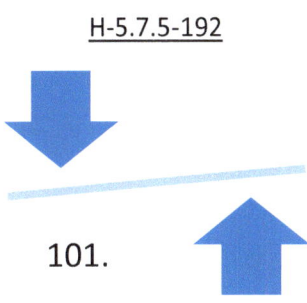

101.

I have no more dreams

Dreams are for sucka ass punks

Sell drugs get money

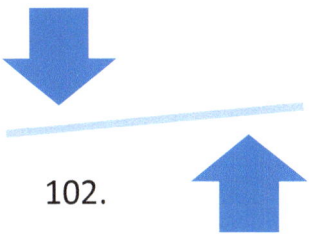

102.

I can't fuck hookers

Why do they sell their body

Is all I think of

Haikus By Michael Irvin Walker

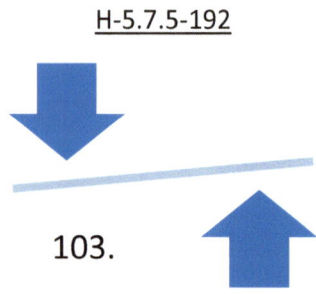

103.

Why do I create

I don't know it keeps me sane

Wish you were dead hoe

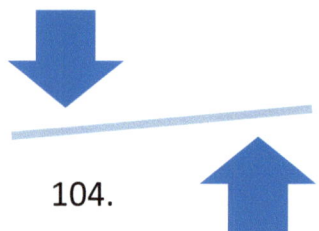

104.

There was a protest

Looting and everything

Rest in peace George Floyd

Haikus By Michael Irvin Walker

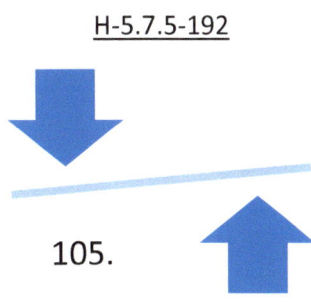

105.

Why do people loot

Looting is not protesting

So please don't do it

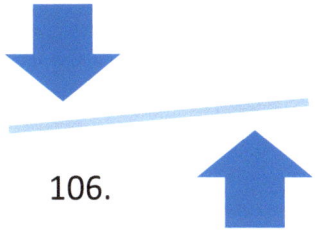

106.

People are angry

ACAB FTP FUCK 12

Written on the streets

Haikus By Michael Irvin Walker

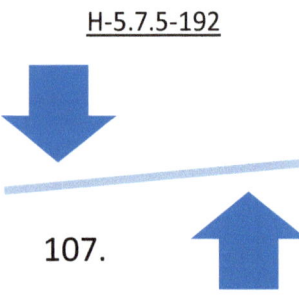

107.

The hate that hate made

White people started this shit

Oh now you're sorry

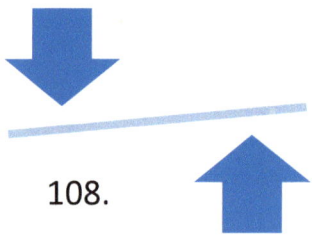

108.

Too late for that shit

Should have said that years ago

So guess what fuck you

Haikus By Michael Irvin Walker

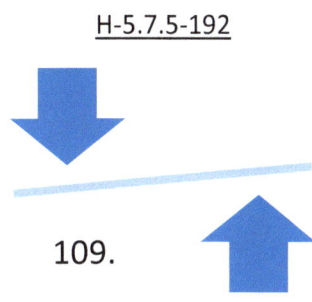

109.

Had a crush on you

Vanessa Bell Calloway

Then you got married

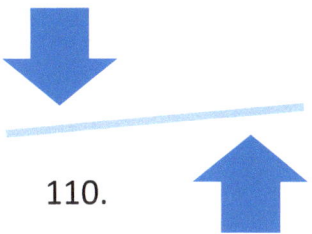

110.

Oh Suzanne Douglas

Such a beautiful woman

Wonder where art thou

Haikus By Michael Irvin Walker

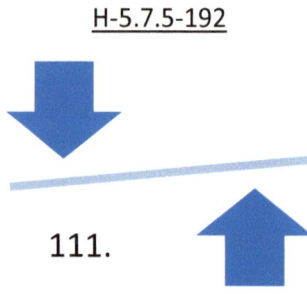

111.

A whole lot has changed

We ain't our ancestors

We will fuck you up

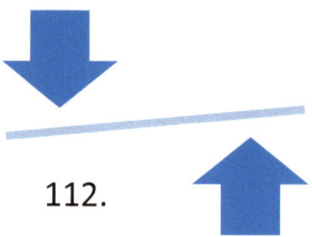

112.

All the things you do

Nothing ever comes from it

So what is the use

Haikus By Michael Irvin Walker

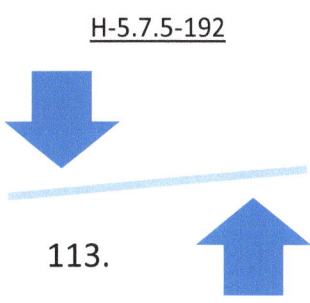

113.

Love is hard to find

Think you're in love then you're not

Just have great sex then

114.

I am getting old

Time cannot be defeated

Gray hairs all over

Haikus By Michael Irvin Walker

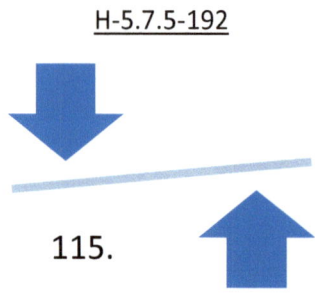

115.

Today is Thursday

We buried George Floyd today

Today is so sad

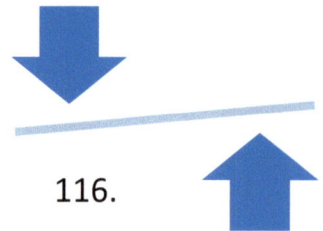

116.

I'm telling you now

If verdict is not guilty

We'll burn this bitch down

Haikus By Michael Irvin Walker

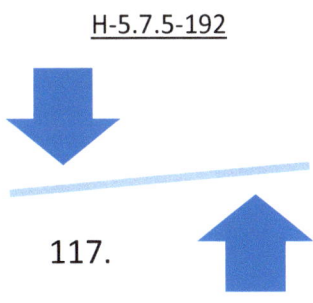

117.

Oh he not guilty

King Kong ain't got shit on me

You watch what happen

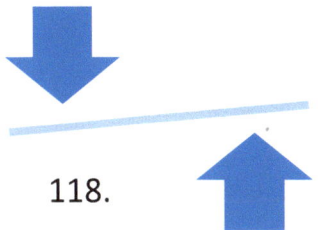

118.

I dare you fuckers

Try me I'm not bullshittin'

Yes this is a test

Haikus By Michael Irvin Walker

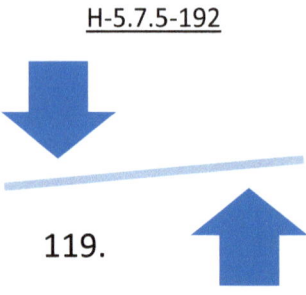

119.

On the name George Floyd

Not playin' mutha fuckaz

We'll see verdict day

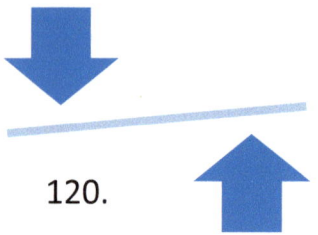

120.

Radio Raheem

It's police brutality

We changing this shit

Haikus By Michael Irvin Walker

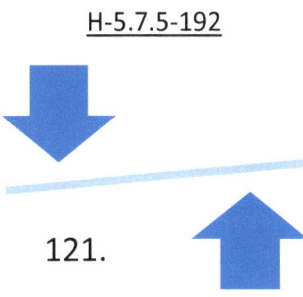

121.

The bars are open

We can take off the mask now

Corona bullshit

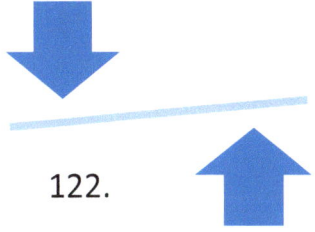

122.

Need new direction

The way I'm movin' ain't it

Got to switch it up

Haikus By Michael Irvin Walker

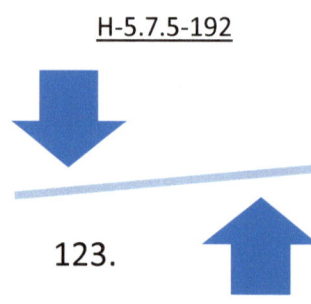

123.

Just look at your ass

Never had to overcome

You pompous punk prick

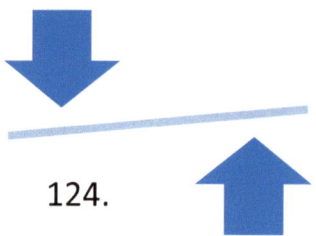

124.

I'm a smart nigga

I'm going to harvard u

Why not howard u

Haikus By Michael Irvin Walker

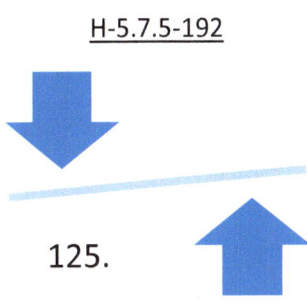

125.

Living life for dreams

Dreams never seem to come true

Fuck it stop dreaming

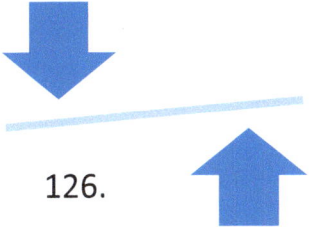

126.

Wonder if BIG's dream

Fucking an R&B bitch

If ever he did

Haikus By Michael Irvin Walker

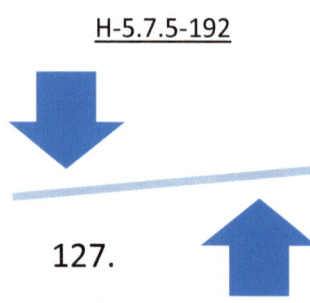

127.

I'm so sick of her

But I can't get rid of her

She is a nympho

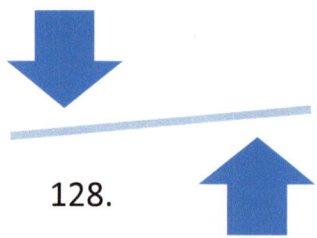

128.

What if I told you

Maybe it's best I do not

I cannot trust you

Haikus By Michael Irvin Walker

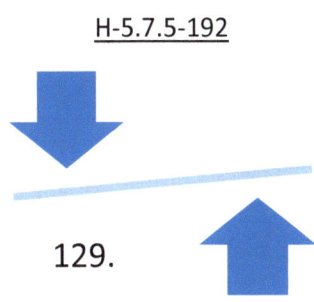

129.

Listen to me good

WTF are you doing

Stop that shit right now

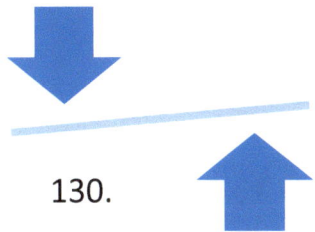

130.

What technology

It is like a black mirror

That thing will kill you

Haikus By Michael Irvin Walker

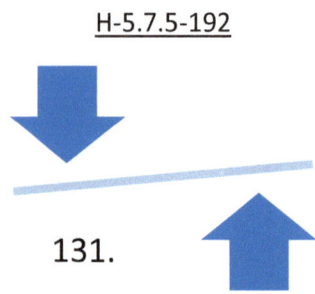

131.

Netflix is feces

Just a bunch of old movies

I'll deactivate

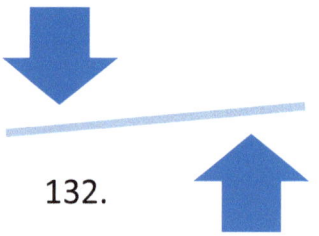

132.

I have hit a wall

Just can't do it anymore

You have to check out

Haikus By Michael Irvin Walker

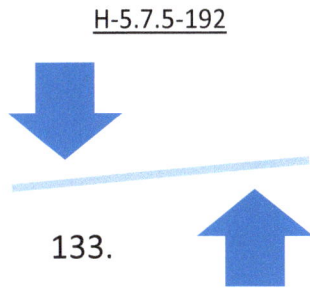

133.

Anytime you want

It ain't gonna be easy

I'm ready for you

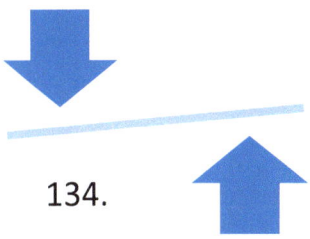

134.

It is important

What's the focus of your time

Please do not waste mine

Haikus By Michael Irvin Walker

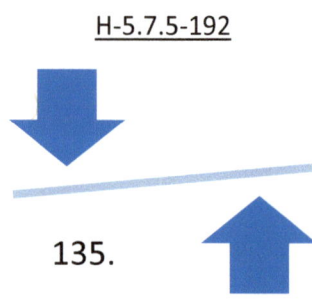

135.

That's KRS ONE

So you're a philosopher

Yes that would be me

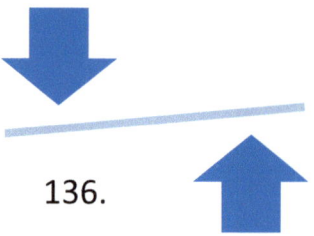

136.

The science of blood

What it means to be a dad

He is I am him

Haikus By Michael Irvin Walker

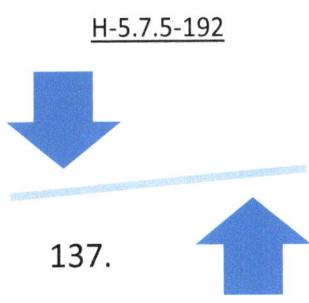

137.

Was so damn funky

Parliament Funkadelic

I miss George Clinton

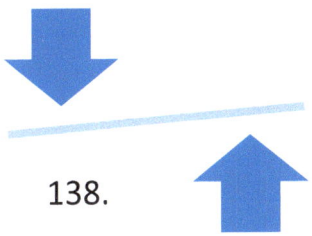

138.

The gyms are open

Have not worked out in six mths

It is June fifteenth

Haikus By Michael Irvin Walker

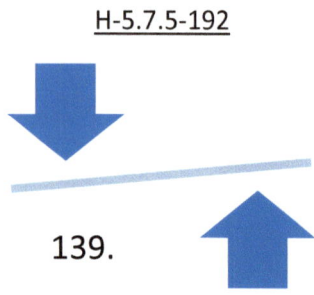

139.

Being single is

I'm both too old and too young

I can't find a wife

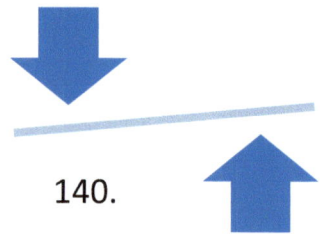

140.

Amaud Arbery

George Floyd Rashard Brooks God Damn

Will it ever end

Haikus By Michael Irvin Walker

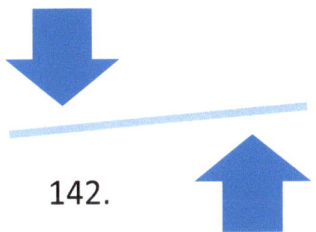

141.

I'm forty seven

I will never stop rappin'

HIP HOP TILL I DIE

142.

That's Charlie Parker

Greatest saxophone player

For eva eva

Haikus By Michael Irvin Walker

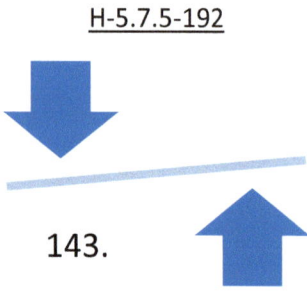

143.

Don't know what I want

Maybe I don't want nothin'

Yeah that's what I want

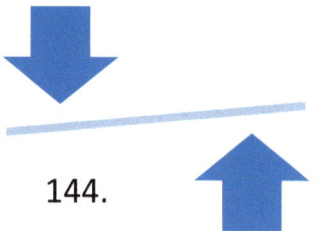

144.

That there is Sure Sure

The Beatles to funky beats

That's why I like them

Haikus By Michael Irvin Walker

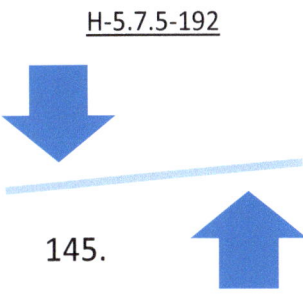

145.

Time for civil war

Get your guns ready to shoot

Shoot white men on sight

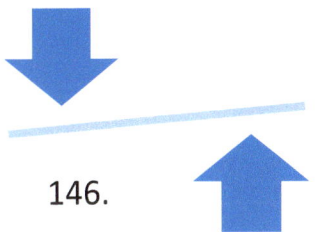

146.

Summer is over

Hope covid-19 is too

2020 GO

Haikus By Michael Irvin Walker

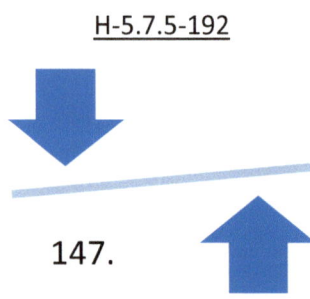

147.

You live long enough

You will meet some cool people

You may become friends

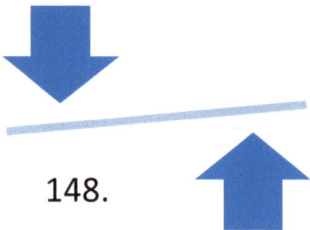

148.

You want more haikus

I can't think of anything

I will be right back

Haikus By Michael Irvin Walker

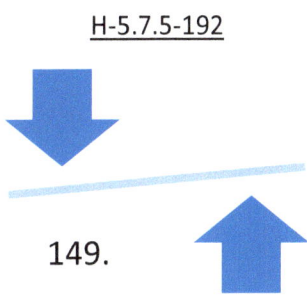

149.

It is so crazy

The better you are the more

Your friends will hate you

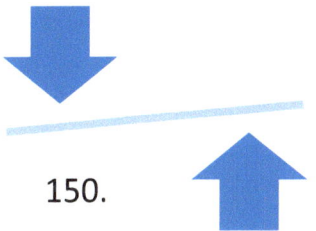

150.

Weed is legal now

Been smoking a lot lately

It is the Cali

Haikus By Michael Irvin Walker

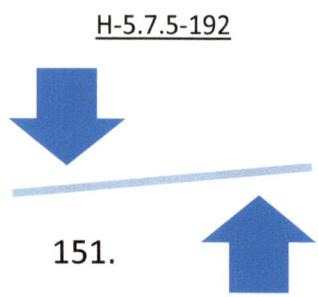

151.

Labor day weekend

Just saw K.D. on the beach

I was high as hell

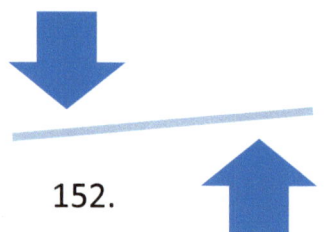

152.

I really don't know

What the fuck I am doing

Please just be present

Haikus By Michael Irvin Walker

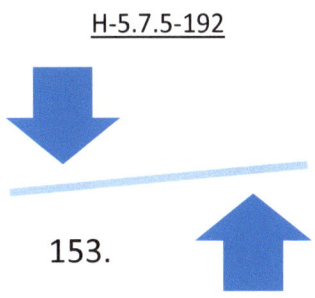

153.

She sends videos

Almost like being with her

I jerk off to them

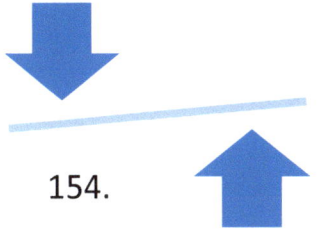

154.

I'm ready for love

Just can't find a sexy bitch

Yo man fuck these hoes

Haikus By Michael Irvin Walker

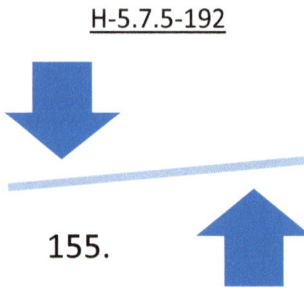

155.

Women can't play chest

Tell that to Elizabeth

Check mate you bastard

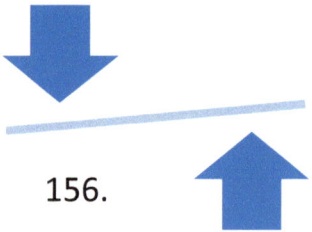

156.

I'm saving money

Fourteen thousand one hundred

That's how much I got

Haikus By Michael Irvin Walker

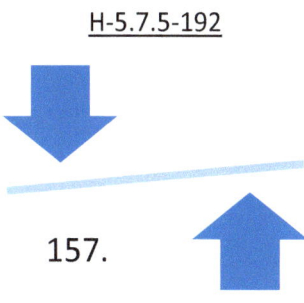

157.

Please put on a thong

Panty lines are disgusting

See you look better

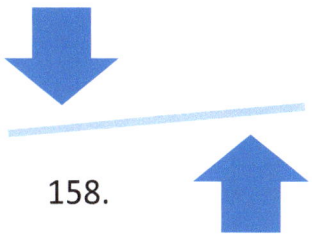

158.

You think you're stylish

Wearing tight dress and tight jeans

That is not great style

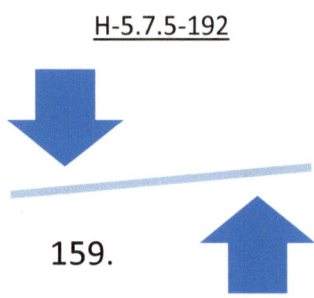

159.

My mother is like

You're educated but dumb

She wants to be me

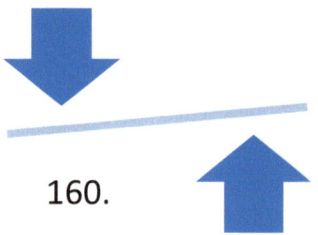

160.

I don't like my boss

Maryann is the worst boss

Time for a new boss

Haikus By Michael Irvin Walker

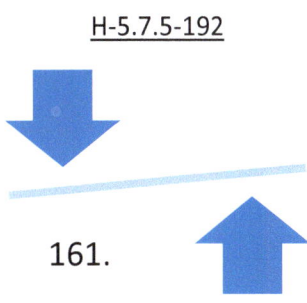

161.

A surprise party

For my cousins' 50th

His wife fucked it up

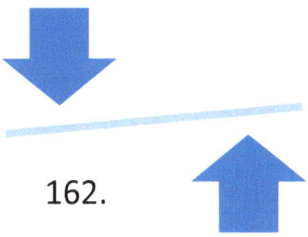

162.

They say I'm handsome

But that shit don't mean nothing

Can't get a sexy…

Haikus By Michael Irvin Walker

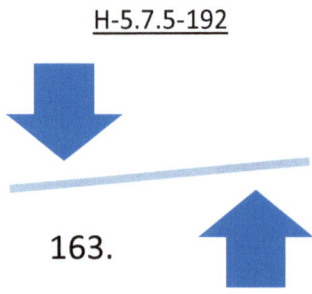

163.

On hinge dating app

Results are disappointing

Scared of the Black Man

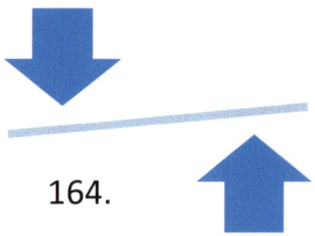

164.

White people won't stop

Are naturally racist

In their DNA

Haikus By Michael Irvin Walker

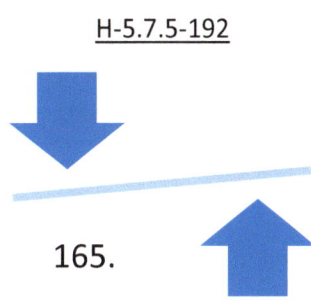

165.

Asians are racist

I interviewed at Stiiizy

All Asians no job

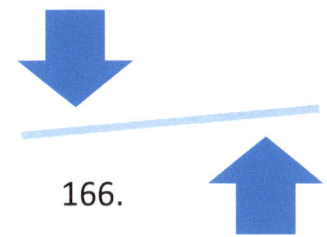

166.

Got money in stocks

Was up ten thousand dollars

Now only up four

Haikus By Michael Irvin Walker

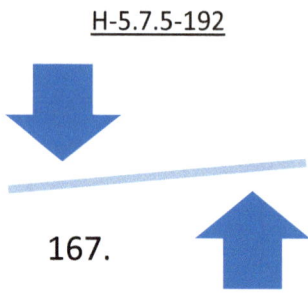

167.

I'm not feeling well

Me feeling lorn and lonely

Go fuck a hooker

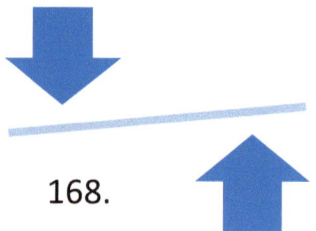

168.

Megan the stallion

Women in LA are hoes

I hate Loriale

Haikus By Michael Irvin Walker

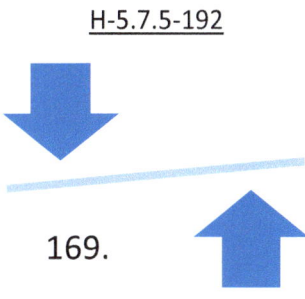

169.

Racist white people

In the park in my own car

Park ranger walks up

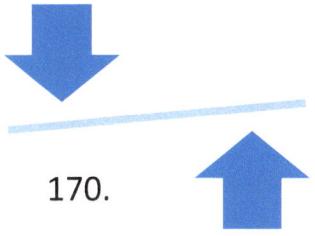

170.

Trying to lose weight

Stomach looks ridiculous

I am at the gym

Haikus By Michael Irvin Walker

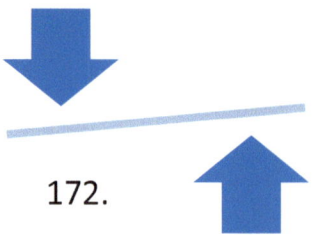

171.

Valentina has

An agenda to use me

To move to Cali

172.

She says she wants to

Moving to California

Using me to move

Haikus By Michael Irvin Walker

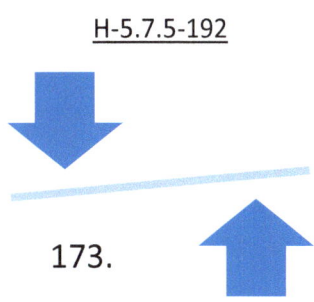

173.

I quit drinking beer

Been smoking a lot of weed

And drinking more wine

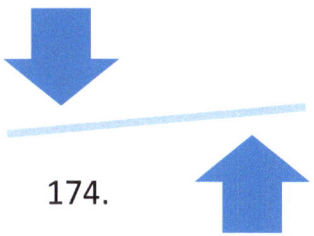

174.

She visited me

I orgasmed hard and loud

I missed that pussy

Haikus By Michael Irvin Walker

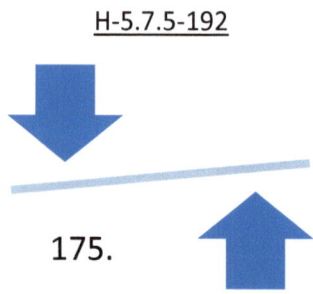

175.

Try not to be bored

A lot of time in one day

Don't sweat the technique

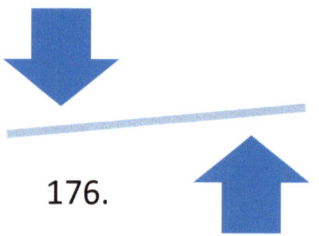

176.

Me, narcissistic

You're just a jealous dumb rube

And you're insecure

Haikus By Michael Irvin Walker

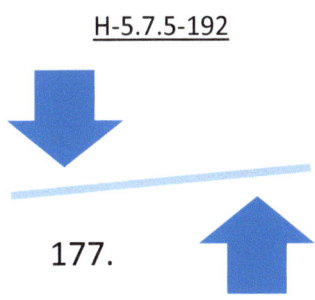

177.

No rhyme or reason

Just be happy with yourself

God cannot save you

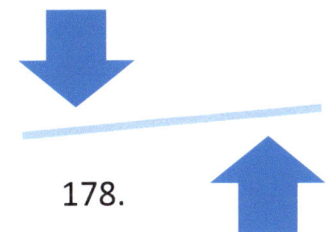

178.

Living your best life

In denial a little

Not how you planned it

Haikus By Michael Irvin Walker

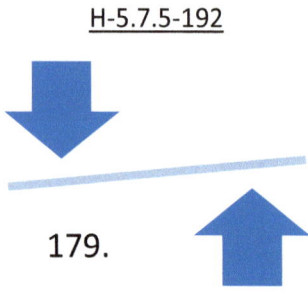

179.

What will happen next

Why would you worry on it

You don't like surprise

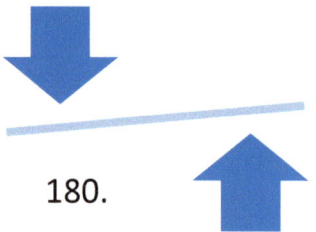

180.

White men have it all

Steve jobs was an idiot

But he got his way

Haikus By Michael Irvin Walker

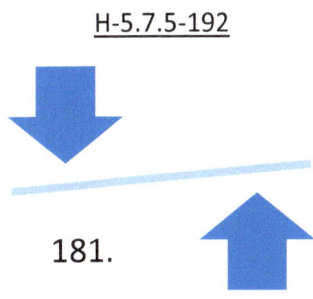

181.

Kilburn Media

Fuck Maryann silly bitch

Systemic racist

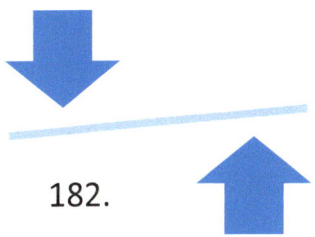

182.

Creativity

I'm goin' all in this bitch

No fear fuck raw dogg

Haikus By Michael Irvin Walker

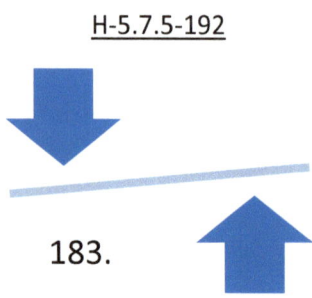

183.

Y'all can't fuck with this

Write rap act and voice over

Shut up and dribble

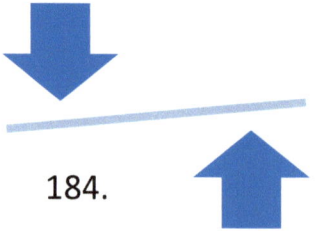

184.

I do love nice hips

And tidys and ass and legs

Thank god for bitches

Haikus By Michael Irvin Walker

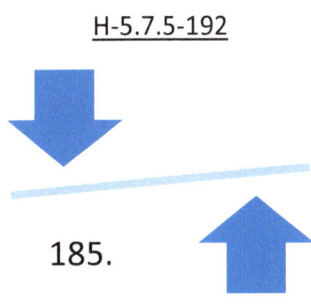

185.

Fuck accounting work

White women are CFOs

No place for black man

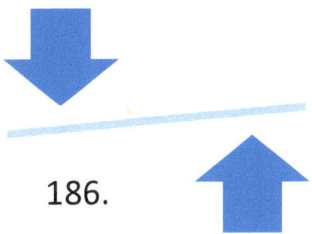

186.

This shit is boring

But I'm a family man

Fuck monogamy

Haikus By Michael Irvin Walker

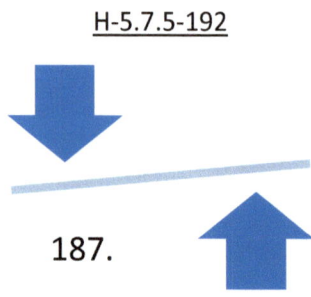

187.

Rapper DMX

In heaven get at me dogg

Hell is hot and dark

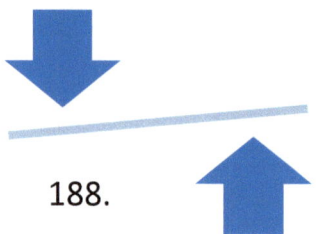

188.

Only Biz Markie

But you say he's just a friend

She caught the vapors

Haikus By Michael Irvin Walker

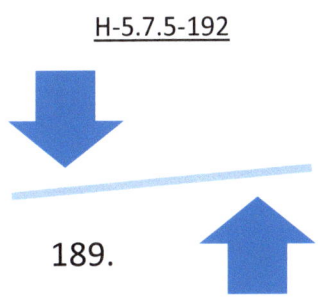

189.

Paul Mooney the best

One nigga two nigga three

Funniest Comic

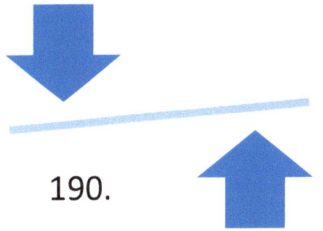

190.

I was a boy once

I cannot remember when

I need therapy

Haikus By Michael Irvin Walker

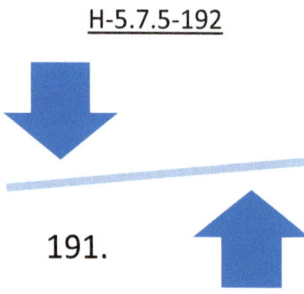

191.

The world is fucked up

Where is the love for dark skin

We gon' be here bitch

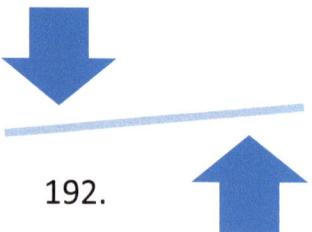

192.

Ain't goin' nowhere

P. Diddy is an icon

The black man is god

Haikus By Michael Irvin Walker

NOTES:

21 inspired by Rapper Teflon, Song "Get Mine", Album "My Will", 1997.

24 inspired by D-Nice hit Hip Hop song "Call Me D-Nice", Album "Call Me D-Nice" 1990. D-Nice's Club Quarantine which the rapper created during the Corona Virus pandemic "Stay-at-home" mandate .

25 inspired by Guy song "Tease Me Tonight", Album "The Future" 1990.

29 inspired as an ode to Hip Hop. Specifically, Showbiz & AG and their Song "Soul Clap", Album "Run Away Slave" 1992. Real Hip Hop respects authenticity, not riches/fame.

35 & 39 inspired by the Hip Hop artist SheReal whom I came across at an Al Sharpton National Action Network (NAN) conference 2014. Listening to her two albums in 2020 (especially the songs THOT Pocket, The Truth, Beautiful Day) inspired me to start rapping again. Cause she makes it very clear that REAL HIP HOP SPOKEN LYRICISM THAT ACTUALLY SAYS SOMETHING IS VERY MUCH ALIVE.

37 inspired by Hip Hop artist NOTORIOS B.I.G. Song "My Downfall", Album "Life After Death" 1997.

Haikus By Michael Irvin Walker

40 The Haiku is specifically
Named "Ahmads' Haiku" in the
name of Ahmad Arbery; first
line inspired by artist Prince,
Song "Dear Mr. Man", Album
"Musicology" 2004; second and
third lines are ire over Ahmad's
murder, that this killing of
black men must stop.

43 inspired by Hip Hop artist
Dynasty, Song "Fly With Me",
Album "DY Forever" 2016.
Dynasty is authentically
Queens New York and I've
always had a proclivity toward
New York MCs and their
delivery of rhyme style; like
hers on this song. This album
also inspired me, specifically
this song, to rap again. Cause
my corporate job life was
exactly as she said "THAT
OTHER THING KEEP BORIN
YOU SO LET IT GO MAN!"

Haikus By Michael Irvin Walker

53 inspired by the film director Spike Lee. For me, he is the progenitor of 1989 and beyond, quality Black Cultural Film story telling.

72 inspired by Derrick Chauvin killing George Floyd; looking like he was living the america dream while doing it, and after, had no worry in the world.

75 & 76, 78, 79, 81 inspired by the NetFlix Michael Jordan special "The Last Dance". Just watching that; even though LeBron has more points and better stats, HE DOESN'T HAVE MORE KILLER MOMENTS THAN MICHAEL JORDAN NOR MORE CHAMPIONSHIPS.

85 inspired by the movie "Goodfellas" 1990.

Haikus By Michael Irvin Walker

90, 91, 92, 93, 94, 95, 97
inspired by four trips in two
years to Moorhead/Indianola
Mississippi to four funerals of
four family members. Roxanna
May is my great grandmother.

104-108 inspired by 5.31.2021
into morning of 6.1.2021 Los
Angeles Melrose Ave George
Floyd Looting Protest Riot.

110 inspired by actress
Suzanne Douglas; weird thing
about this haikus is that she
died a little while after I wrote
this.

111 inspired by 5.31.2022 into
morning of 6.1.2021 Los
Angeles Melrose Ave George
Floyd Looting Protest Riot. A
young lady had a sign that said
this in non-haiku form.

Haikus By Michael Irvin Walker

115 was written on the day GEORGE Floyd was buried.

116-120 inspired by Derrick Chauvin, George Floyd murderer court case. If the verdict was not guilty, I was driving to Minneapolis to protest. I was definitely going to jail or dying a martyr that weekend. I cried when the verdict was announced and immediacy left work. I was relieved I didn't have to ruin my life for justice. 2nd line of 117 is the famous line spoken by Denzel Washington in his Oscar Winning Performance in the movie Training Day.

118 was inspired by Derrick Chauvin George Floyd murderer court case. But the 2nd line is inspired by Que talkin' to Bishop in the movie "Juice".

Haikus By Michael Irvin Walker

135 inspired by Boogie Down Productions Rapper KRSONE Song "My Philosophy", Album "By All Means Necessary" 1988.

137 inspired by George Clinton and Parliament Funkadelic who made some the most original funk music in history.

145 if the police and whomever else, such as George Zimmerman continue to blatantly kill black men, even on camera, without Justice being served, there will be a racial civil war in America.

187 inspired by DMX death announcement. He had a great impact on Hip Hop.

Haikus By Michael Irvin Walker

188 inspired by the death announcement of Hip Hop: Beatbox, Artist and DJ, Biz Markie.

189 inspired by the death announcement of Paul Mooney. Though I do not promulgate the use of the word "nigga" except in art and Hip Hop Music; that word is inseparable from Paul Mooney; a great comedic artist.

www.ingramcontent.com/pod-product-compliance
Lightning Source LLC
Chambersburg PA
CBHW040904120626
46551CB00006B/632

* 9 7 9 8 9 8 5 9 1 5 6 2 4 *